The Positive

Psychology Diet:

21 Days to a Happier

and Healthier Life

Gemma Nastasi

ISBN: 1517383633

ISBN 13: 9781517383633

To my mother, June Anita Aliotta.

May she rest in peace.

Are you ready to change your life for the better?

We are all connected, and the universal language is a smile.

Acknowledgement

I am so grateful for all the wonderful people in my life. I have truly been blessed. Thank you to my family and friends. Your support has been instrumental in my life. I love you all!

Contents

Contents	
Introduction	1
The Days Begin	13
Day One—The Breath of Life, Gratitude,	28
Day Two—Gratitude	46
Day Three—Mindfulness	48
Day Four—Savor	50
Day Five—Nutrition, Exercise, and Sleep	52
Day Six—Words and Assumptions	65
Day Seven—Play, Smile, and Hug	68
Day Eight—Opportunity and Luck	76
Day Nine—Character	79
Day Ten—Reframing Thoughts	82
Day Eleven—Regret: Reversible and	85
Day Twelve—Relationships and Love	87
Day Thirteen—Flow	94
Day Fourteen—Intuition and	96
Day Fifteen—Fear	100
Day Sixteen—Organization	103
Day Seventeen—Visualization	105
Day Eighteen—Converting Emotional Pain and Forgiveness	108
Day Nineteen—Life's Purpose	114
Day Twenty—Random Acts of Kindness and Volunteer Work	116
Day Twenty-One—Vitality	122
We Are All Connected	124
Live a Hopeful Life	132

Introduction

During most of my childhood, I remember my parents talking about being on a diet. The whole family struggled with dieting, trying to follow whatever new fad diet was on the market. At the beginning of a new diet, I saw their strict observance and excitement about the prospect of losing weight. Unfortunately, that phase was short lived. Within a couple of weeks, I saw them cheating on their diets and observed the guilt and frustration that followed. Sometimes they lost weight and kept it off for a while—only to regain the weight and more in the months ahead. I also observed the eating disorders that developed due to the inability to stick to a diet. There was starvation, bingeing, purging, and finally prescription drugs.

This vicious cycle haunted me throughout my young life.

One definition of "diet" is "to regulate oneself for better health." All the definitions I have found relate diet to food. Although I do not like the word "diet," I use it in the title of this book, because I want the millions of dieters to read this book in the hope that they may stop looking for a magic diet and start the journey toward a happy and healthy life by making positive, healthy changes.

My name is Gemma Nastasi, and I am a certified holistic nutrition coach and a positive-psychology practitioner. I am very fortunate in that I have always been health conscious. I have always understood that food is the fuel that nourishes our body. Many foods have healthy nutrients that help with healing and prevent disease. Food is so important to our body that it astounds me that nutrition courses are not part of the mandatory curriculum in public schools.

My work as a nutrition coach made me realize that poor self-care is a symptom of a much larger problem. My approach is to listen to what my clients say about themselves. I observed that most had self-esteem issues and were overwhelmed with their stressful lives. Unfortunately, the last thing they had time to focus on was what they were eating. I cringed when I listened to their negative opinion of themselves. It made me realize that their negative thinking and comments had been going on for years. I wanted to get to the bottom of the problem. You must be ready to change to make positive improvements in your life. Thus, the teacher comes when the student is ready. My life's purpose became clear, and I began the journey by learning everything I could about the mind-body connection. The bottom line is that your brain is responsible for everything, and your thoughts mold everything in your world.

If you need balance and direction in your life, whether it is for weight loss, habit change, or just becoming a more positive person, then you will benefit from the tools in this book.

This book has found its way into your hands for a reason. I can assure you that if you

make these positive changes and live by them for 21 days, you will be happier and therefore healthier.

Enjoy the 21-day journey!

Welcome to the World of Positivity

LIFE SATISFACTION WHEEL

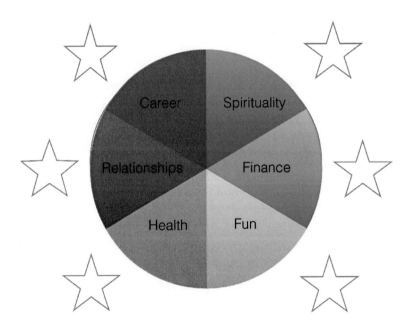

Rate each category with a number value from 1-10
(10 being the greatest satisfaction)

Put your number in the corresponding star.

Gemma Health Coach, LLC
gemma@gemmahealthcoach.com

There are several life-changing events that stick out in my mind and remind me that angels are on earth. When I was twenty-six years old, I worked in a real-estate office as an agent. The manager, Jack, was not particularly fond of me. Jack was an older man in his late seventies, and he had had polio as a child. He walked with crutches and obviously had a hard life. I had the feeling that he thought that I was a spoiled little rich girl and that my life had been easy. It was no secret that my father was a very successful real-estate investor. He owned a valuable piece of property that could be developed for townhouses and asked me to find him a buyer. I worked with another agent in my office, who produced a very qualified buyer. We all met at my father's office to discuss the property with the buyer and Jack. A deal was made, and the commission was going to be $700,000. Since I was working on it with another agent in my office, I stood to make $175,000. That money would have changed my life. Everything was going smoothly with the contract until the attorney review process began. The attorney called my manager and said that the sellers (my father and his partner) refused to pay the commission. When my manager called my father, my father ridiculed him and told him he was stupid not to get a signed commission agreement. My manager replied by telling my father, "Your daughter works here, and we trusted that you would want your daughter to benefit from getting a commission." Later my father called me to tell me that my manager was in his office and that he did not get a commission agreement signed; therefore, he and his friends would not pay a commission. Needless to say I was devastated.

Shortly after that, I got a call from my manager requesting to see me in his office. I hoped that he would not see that I had been crying. I was preparing to be fired. The ride to the office was torture. I felt ashamed and embarrassed for my father's actions. I was telling myself that my manager did not like me and he was probably going to say, "The apple doesn't fall far from the tree." The only positive thought was that at least it was the end of the day, and not many people would be in the office to see me get fired. I did not blame the manager; I was convinced that I deserved to be fired by association with my father and his actions.

The office was quiet when I arrived. My manager called my name and asked me to enter his semiprivate workstation. The only thing holding back my tears was the lump in my throat. I sat down quietly as he proceeded to tell me the news about the commission that I already knew. The pain of hearing it again was excruciating; however, I was aware that he had to tell me why he was letting me go. The conversation took a shift, though, when I told him how sorry I was and that I did not blame him for firing me. I deserved it. My tears flowed. His reaction shocked me. He said he would never fire me. He told me that he had contracted polio as a child. His parents were told that he needed to be in an institution for the rest of his life. He said that he

had a wife and two daughters, that he had a house

and a family, and that he had supported his family

in a comfortable way all these years. He then told

me the most valuable thing that anyone had ever

told me: "You don't have to play with the cards you

are dealt with. You can change things. Do not accept

what you do not want." At that moment, I knew

that my difficult life had flashed in front of Jack's

eyes. He beckoned me into his arms to accept the

warm hug that I desperately needed. We both cried

as I turned the page to create the life that I wanted.

This book is not going to be another memoir of a

tragic life, describing the pain and suffering that

followed. Nor is it going to be about the "learned

helplessness" that kept me locked in a very

unhappy life for forty-nine years. This book has
come about due to my many years of suffering,
during which I also observed the emotional
suffering of my loved ones. I am truly grateful that I
had the advantage of being born with a very
positive outlook so that I had the strength to
overcome the negativity. Emotional pain can come
from unsuccessful dieting, an unhappy marriage,
divorce, loneliness, and loss of any sort, just to name
a few.

Although some unhappiness is healthy, ruminating
on it is not. The misconception that existed in my
childhood was that weight loss would bring
happiness. I agree that feeling better about your
appearance is an important ingredient in a happy

life, but you have to change your life in all areas and achieve balance.

As I look back to my early years, I realize that the emotional pain I experienced and witnessed was no accident. It was the seed that I cultivated into my life's purpose of helping others achieve happier and healthier lives.

The Days Begin

Positivity

Positivity: Positive emotions that bring out optimal happiness, flourish, and flow

Happiness: The emotion that makes you feel great.

Flourishing: The optimal range of functioning, which signifies goodness, growth and resilience.

Flow (zone): The mental state of operation in which a person is fully energized and involved so that enjoyment and happiness are evident during any task.

What Is Positive Psychology?

Martin Seligman is a psychologist, educator, and author. He is also the founder of positive psychology. His self-help books and philosophy on positivity have turned the world of psychology around by focusing on all that is right with a person and his or her life rather than what is wrong.

The purpose of this book is to increase well-being by utilizing the tools of positive psychology.

Why 21 Days?

Maxwell Meltz was a plastic surgeon in the 1950s. He observed habits and changes among his patients as well as in himself and concluded that it took twenty-one days for an old mental image to dissolve and a new one to form.

Going forward, the theory estimated it would take anywhere from two to eight months to change behavior or form a new habit. It was also concluded that if you happened to make mistakes along the road to change, those mistakes would not have an effect on your long-term goal.

If you can adapt these positive changes in your life for twenty-one days, then you will have created a foundation for a new life.

You Can Increase Your Happiness!

A study by Dr. Sonja Lyubomirsky has shown that 50 percent of our happiness is genetic and out of our control, 10 percent of our happiness results from life satisfaction, and 40 percent is controllable. The great news is we have at least 40 percent to work with. Anything more is great!

New-Life Supplies

Life-satisfaction wheel – Make copies on page 5

Calendar

Notebook

Pen

Poster board

Markers

Crayons

Glue stick

Favorite photo of you at the best time in your life

Magazines (to cut out pictures for a vision board)

Mirror

Shoebox

Life-Satisfaction Wheel

Make a few copies of the life-satisfaction wheel on page

5. Before you read the rest of this book, fill out the life-

satisfaction wheel. Place a number from one to ten in each corresponding star to rate your satisfaction in that area of your life (ten being the number for the highest level of satisfaction). At the end of each week, fill out another wheel, and track your progress in each area. This practice will act as a guide to keep you aware of the weaknesses and strengths in your life.

Calendar

Congratulations! You are starting your journey to a happier and healthier life! I am so happy that I can help you achieve your goals.

You deserve to be happy and healthy!

Today is the first day of your new life!

Find a place to prominently display your calendar. Draw a small happy face and put a number one (1) next to it.

Each day you will mark your calendar with a happy face

until you reach the twenty-one-day mark. You can continue marking your calendar after twenty-one days if you choose. This is your life, and these are your rules.

Daily Journal

It is best to write in your journal at bedtime. Get your notebook, and mark number one on the first page. This is your daily gratitude journal. Leave the journal on your bed in the morning so that you remember to write in it in the evening before bedtime.

Vision Board

It is arts and crafts time. You can be as creative as you want. Take out your poster board and supplies. Cut out pictures. Post pictures of a time when you felt you were at your best. Post pictures of your hopes and dreams. Hang it next to your calendar and view it every day.

Savoring Bank

This is your creation. It can be a poster board or shoebox where you post special memories that bring you joy. Place pictures inside the shoebox, and decorate the box with all of your special memories. Let the positive energy flow!

Meditation Place

Find a comfortable place in your house, office, or outdoors to meditate at the same time every day. Make the space your spiritual sanctuary. Light candles and burn incense if you wish. This is your place and your time. Enjoy!

Tools for Happiness and to Increase Life Satisfaction

Spirituality—recognize the higher power, and trust that it will guide you if you look for and follow the signs

Gratitude—write daily gratitude lists

Relationships (family, friends, coworkers, romantic partner)—nurture and appreciate your relationships; repair existing ones, and build new, positive ones

Goals—set goals, and write them down

Achievement—achieve your goals and dreams

Kindness—be kind to yourself and others

Flow—the natural progression that energizes you and brings you joy

Optimism—think positively

Forgiveness—forgive yourself and others; let go of the pain

Savor—be mindful of your surroundings and appreciate the good for twenty seconds; this will help to create new, positive pathways to the brain.

Meditation—relax and breathe

Visualization—visualize the present or future the way you want it to be

Volunteer—give the gift of your time to help others;

perform acts of kindness

Focus on the good by reframing negative thoughts.

Gratitude

We have all heard the old phrase, "Count your blessings."

In today's world, we often lose sight of the things that we

should be grateful for. Perhaps it is not our fault. Our

brains are wired for negativity. In fact, it takes three

positive things or events to cancel out one negative event.

The bottom line is that our brain controls everything. In

order to understand how the brain processes information,

I am going to talk in very simple terms about a few parts

of the very complex brain.

The Brain

Although the brain has many parts and controls the entire body, I am only going to give a brief overview of some parts of the brain in order to understand our thinking process.

The "reptilian brain," or the "lizard brain," is the part of the brain that we share with animals. Its functions are as follows: fight, flight, feeding, and fornication. When an event happens, the information is processed by the reptilian brain first. It then automatically sends out a fight, flight, feeding, or fornication response. This brain response was developed by our ancestors, because they had to rely on these responses to survive.

Over time, the neocortex was formed. The neocortex, or the "human brain," is known as the *new* brain. It is responsible for processing information and problem solving. This new brain makes decisions based on social cues and helps us interpret what others think.

The limbic system, or the "mouse brain," is the part of the brain that supports long-term memory and also a wider range of emotions. It allows us to learn from our own experiences and anticipate danger instead of just reacting to it.

Word of advice: Sleep on it!

If you react suddenly, you will probably be reacting from your lizard brain, and it will probably be the wrong reaction. Take a few minutes or hours to think things over; think overnight, if you can do so. It will help you to properly process the situation before reacting.

Mind Chatter

We have all heard of many books about the law of attraction. Although these books are inspirational, they do not tell you how to change your thoughts. They just tell you that you must change your thoughts in order to change your life. This is true—but how can you do that?

Positive psychology: It offers you tools and techniques to help with the transformation to positive thinking and living.

What is mind chatter? It is the way your mind processes information and the self-talk that follows. The way you talk to yourself molds your life. Your thoughts create your world. If you are typically a negative person, it would follow that you could expect very negative self-talk. Be mindful of your thoughts, and try to have a growth mindset whenever possible. Talk back to your thoughts. Use the kind of words that you would use when you talk to a dear friend. You will be opening the door to a much more exciting world through your thoughts.

Allow yourself to be human: How do you do that? There are three ways to do so: self-awareness, self-compassion, and self-care. We are not robots. We have to take care of our mental and physical health. When you get physically hurt, you take care of the wound. Similarly, the emotional hurts need care too. Check in daily to evaluate how you are feeling (mentally and physically). Be kind to yourself and practice self-care.

Do you have a fixed mindset or a growth mindset? A fixed mindset is the thought process that believes that our character, intelligence, and how we measure up are fixed.

It leads us to believe that we can only achieve what we are capable of and avoid challenges.

A growth mindset thrives on challenges and sees failures as stepping stones to success and growth.

Your mindset affects your life through your thoughts. Your job and your relationships are the results of your mindset. You are what you think.

Do you have a fixed mindset or a growth mindset? Do you like the results you get when you have a fixed mindset? Try changing your mindset to a growth mindset on some things that are not important. Observe the results.

Satisficer or Maximizer: Are you a satisficer or maximizer? A satisificer is satisfied and makes decisions easily when his or her criteria are met. A maximizer is always looking to make the optimal decision. He or she examines every option and researches everything before

making a decision.

Most people are a little of both. If you like the way you

make decisions and it works for you, then do not change a

thing. If you struggle and have difficulty making

decisions, then try a new approach.

Just something to think about...

Day One—The Breath of Life, Gratitude, and Habits

Today is the first day of the rest of your new life. Start your day with meditation.

Meditation is a powerful way of connecting with your inner self. You have all that you need within yourself. Focus on each day by living in the present moment. The past is over; if you revert to the past, you will freeze in your present life and will not enjoy the gift of each unique day. The future is always changing. We can make plans for our future, but we cannot count on our life evolving according to our plans. The mystery of life can be exciting. Living in the present moment and going with the flow will bring about your ideal life. Using meditation to calm your mind will help you find the right paths to take.

The breathing exercises for meditation and relaxations along with writing a daily gratitude list are the most powerful way to start your first day. Do these two exercises every day for the entire twenty-one days. Even if you follow nothing else in this book, I assure you that you will benefit greatly from focusing on gratitude and de-stressing with breathing.

The Breath of Life

Breathing to De-stress and Relax

Life begins with your first breath and ends with your last breath. Your breath is life and more. You are born with the natural ability to calm yourself with your breath. Upon breathing in and out, you stimulate the vagus nerve, which is connected to the brainstem and extends into the abdomen. This nerve is part of the parasympathetic nervous system.

When your body is stressed by way of the sympathetic nervous system, the fight-or-flight response is activated. Your body has its own way of stress relief by stimulating the vagus nerve through breathing exercises.

As you continue reading the rest of this book, I am sure you will feel more empowered to control your life. You are born with all that you need to cope and survive in your lifetime. Let us start the journey.

Start day one with the following breathing exercise for ten minutes. Our goal is to perform this exercise for twenty minutes a day, but if you have not done breathing exercises on a regular basis, then ten minutes is a good start. Meditate every day for the twenty-one days. I included some meditational practices to help you rid yourself of old memories, hurts, and pain that you may be holding on to. Use the breathing exercise at any time in the twenty-one days as needed.

Meditation has many healing benefits for the mind and body. It is very effective in regard to stress relief and gaining mental clarity, creativity, and so much more.

Daily Breathing Meditation

Go to your comfortable meditation place. It can be in your house or outdoors.

Close your eyes and completely relax your body.

Take a deep breath in and then breathe out slowly. Do this ten times and only concentrate on your breath. Relax every part of your body concentrating on fingers, hands, arms, shoulders, and so on. Feel your body completely relax.

Observe the thoughts that come into your mind and place them on a conveyor belt in front of you. Watch them pass you by.

When you are finished with the breathing meditation, slowly come out of it and open your eyes. You should feel more relaxed. Meditation is like a muscle. You must practice it regularly to reap the benefit.

Clear the Toxins from Your Lungs

Every day we are breathing in unhealthy air. The toxins stay in our lungs. Follow this breathing exercise daily to cleanse your lungs.

Take a Deep Breath

Breathing exercises clear your lungs of stale air and toxins and also release stress. Try it. You have nothing to lose.

Deep Breathing Exercise

Do this cleansing exercise daily for the entire twenty-one days to clear your toxins. Sit in a comfortable position.

Breathe in through your nose as deeply as you can, and when you are done, try to breathe in a little more.

Now hold it for five full seconds.

Then slowly release for five seconds, and when you think you are done releasing your breath, push out a little more.

Repeat this ten times a day and notice how you feel!

Happy Dance

What Is the Happy Dance?

The "happy dance" is letting go and dancing with joy to your favorite song. It is a great way to wake up your body with music and to create a positive start. Music has been proven to elevate moods. Pick a favorite song that makes you feel happy. Stand in front of a mirror to do your own "happy dance" to your favorite song.

My favorite song is *Top of the World*.

Meditation Exercise to Surrender and Release

We all carry problems and burdens daily. These problems and burdens add stress and sadness to our lives. Follow the below steps in your next meditation to release all negative things from your life:

Get into a comfortable position and close your eyes.

Listen to your breath.

Now visualize a big box. Place all the negative things in your life in the box one by one.

Visualize a beautiful card and write a note to send with the box. For example, "Thank you for taking my problems from me; I feel free and happy."

Close the top of the box and tape it up.

Now pick out the most beautiful wrapping paper and wrap and decorate the box.

Decide how you want to transport it. Do you want to put it on a plane, bus, train, car, or boat?

Once you decide how to send it, let go, and watch it leave you.

Feel the peace and relief of letting go. Believe that all the things that you put in the box will work out.

Believe that positive things will come to replace all the negative things that you let go of.

Now smile and do the happy dance and feel the happiness that you deserve.

Do this exercise as many times as you have to in order to feel the peace that comes from the surrender and release.

Goals

Setting goals on day one is a powerful way to work toward a happier and healthier life.

Goals are very important for our happiness. There is a pleasurable sense of achievement upon reaching a goal. Writing down your goals is an effective way of holding yourself accountable. Use the following worksheet to write down your goals.

Goal Setting

Name_____

Date_____

Goal_____

By_____

Write down the action steps that you are taking for the goal.

_____

_____

_____

Write down how you will measure your progress and celebrate your wins.

_____

_____

_____

_____

Write down your primers (reminders and cues). For example, write on your calendar or put helpful messages in your phone reminder and program it to give you a message every couple of days.

Make sure your goal is approachable.

Write down the name of the person or people whom you will count on for accountability (important step for success).

_____

_____

_____

The last step is *commitment*.

Agreement

I, _____, agree to

complete my goal successfully by the date of

_____.

_____   _____

Signature   **Date**

Habits

Day one is the perfect day to work on habit change.
Although I have so much to share with you, I want to add
habits on the first day since it takes twenty-one days for
the brain to start to recognize a habit change. I say "habit
change," because you cannot get rid of a habit; you can
only change it. Some habits are good, such as brushing
your teeth after each meal; and some are bad, such as
biting your nails, eating late at night, smoking, and so on.
Did you know that 40 percent of our actions are habits?
Did you ever wonder what creates a habit? Habits are
created by information being chunked together in the
basal ganglia (a part of the brain). Every time that you
resist a temptation, you create a new pathway in your
brain and strengthen your self-regulation.
Did you know that dopamine (a neurotransmitter that
controls the brain's reward and pleasure centers) gets

released in your brain at the anticipation of a behavior or thing? You do not actually have to do it in order to feel the pleasure.

Changing Bad Habits

Write down the habit that you wish to change.

_____

_____

_____

Write down the craving or trigger for this habit.

_____

_____

_____

Write down the reason why you want to change this habit.

_____

_____

Write down the reward you get from this habit and

how much pleasure you get from this habit.

_____

_____

_____

Now think of something that you can do in place

of this habit.

_____

_____

_____

Write down a new reward. The reward has to be

just as good if not better than the current reward.

Track your progress daily. Try to go at least twenty-one days practicing the new habit in place of the old one. This will form the foundation for the habit change. Do not worry if you falter for a few days. Research has proven that if you fall off the habit change road along the way, it does not ruin the chances of making a positive change. Just resume the new positive habit as soon as you are able to do so.

Thought-Rumination-Habit Example

Thought habit: Rumination over a past romantic relationship that failed

Usually the memory is focused on a happy time in the relationship rather than on viewing the relationship as a whole and the negative things that caused the failure. This can be extremely painful and take years to overcome, unless you start to replace this thought habit with a new one.

Trigger/cue: You see couples who look happy.

Reward: Bittersweet—your brain focuses on a happy memory. This is painful and unhealthy, because the reality is that the relationship is no longer a part of your life.

Replacement thought: When the thought of the past romantic relationship comes into your mind, repeat these words to yourself, "I am now open and free for the right person to come in. I am in a much better position and place to accept the love that is on the way, the love I deserve." Close your eyes and feel the love surrounding you. Wrap your arms around yourself, and give yourself a hug to feel the self-love. That is the most important love of all. When you truly love yourself, you will be ready for someone else to come into your life.

Day Two—Gratitude

Gratitude is powerful! This is my favorite exercise. I really love it, and it will make you happier, if you write down your gratitude list daily. Studies have shown that people who write gratitude lists are happier and remained happier even months after they were not writing the lists anymore.

Get your journal. Every night before you go to bed, write down all the things that you are grateful for. Follow this guide. Do not miss a night. Studies have shown that gratitude lists increase your happiness level.

Write down three things that you are grateful for that happened during your day and how you contributed to the good things happening.

Write down three things that you are grateful for in your life.

Write down three wishes for your future.

Write down three sentences thanking the universe for the future things.

Write down these things as if you have already received them.

Close your eyes and experience the feeling of already having them. Hold that feeling for twenty seconds or longer.

Day Three—Mindfulness

Everyone has heard the expression, "Take time to stop and smell the roses." The New Age version of this saying is to try to be mindful. Live in the present moment. When I was first practicing being mindful, I realized why it is so difficult. I was in my local grocery store, and it was the first week of October. I saw the Christmas decorations being put up. I was confused and had to ask myself what month it was. In this fast-paced world, we are living in the future and forgetting to enjoy the present moment.

Do you ever forget where you parked your car? If you answered yes, then try to practice being mindful the next time you park your car. Stick a Post-it note on the dashboard to remind yourself where you parked your car.

Do you notice the natural beauty around you? Nature is so beautiful, and sometimes we are so preoccupied with our lives that we miss the beauty.

Today is day three of your journey toward a happier and healthy life. Start trying to focus on the present. Take time to appreciate the natural beauty around you. Being mindful takes practice. Start your mindfulness practice today. It will get easier to be mindful the more you practice.

Exercise for mindfulness: Take a walk in nature, and observe all the things around you. Take it in, and feel the beauty. Be in the present moment for at least five minutes.

Other mindful exercises include knitting, sewing, exercising, doing a puzzle, jarring tomatoes, or any task that takes concentration. Practice being mindful each day.

Day Four—Savor

Today is savoring day. Think of a pleasant thought, and hold the thought in your mind for twenty seconds. This will help the mind to recall the savoring thought the next time you want to think of it.

Savoring and mindfulness go together. In order to savor, you have to be mindful of something. Recently, I went on a trip to Mexico. Although I have been fortunate to have traveled a lot, I truly enjoyed this trip more than any trip I have ever taken. The reason is because I savored every moment—from the moment that I left my house until the moment I returned home.

Savoring exercise: Create a pleasurable experience. Think about it for twenty seconds. Feel the pleasure. This memory will be stored in your brain for you to recall when you want a little brain pleasure.

Create your own savoring bank: Get a shoebox or poster board. Glue memorable pictures on the board or put them in the shoebox. If you use a shoebox, you can put other memorable things in the box in addition to these pictures. This special savoring bank will hold your memories that you can view anytime you need a positive boost.

Do not forget to savor your achievement. Feel the pleasure for twenty seconds and praise yourself. Great job!

Did you know that studies have shown that the best gifts to give or get are experiences—gifts of time spent with loved ones doing something special?

Enjoy!

Day Five—Nutrition, Exercise, and Sleep

Throw out your processed foods. If you cannot pronounce the ingredients, then do not eat it. It amazes me that people put expensive gas in their cars to get the best performance, yet they do not properly feed their own bodies.

Make sure you have a rainbow or a variety of fruits and vegetables every day. Eat six times a day in small meals. Eat fresh vegetables and fruits (organic and local), lean meat and fish that are antibiotic and hormone free. Have wild salmon twice a week if you can. *Drink plenty of water, at least eight glasses per day.*

Be mindful of too much starch and sugar. Only eat foods high in starch and sugar in moderation.

Limit your dairy products. Watch your portion sizes. You can be eating all the right foods but eating too much. I am telling you to have the birthday cake when the time arises, just a smaller portion. I do not want you to be sitting at a birthday party looking deprived and unhappy. I want you to balance your life in every area. The key word is moderation. If you add physical activity, adequate sleep, and proper nutrition, then a little birthday cake will not ruin your life.

Did you know that you get the pleasure from seeing the dessert before you eat it? You do not have to actually eat it. Your brain sees in pictures. It is brain candy.

You need to live your life without feeling deprived. That is why I do not like diets. Research shows that most diets do not work in the long term. Most people lose weight only to put it back on and more in the months following the diet.

Since the brain sees in pictures, there is a power to writing things down. It makes you mindful of what you are eating. If you are looking to lose weight or eat healthier, then use your notebook, or "My Food Journal," to write down everything that you eat and drink. This is your private book.

You are born with all that you need to live your life. The power is inside of you.

Stress can cause overeating and binge eating. If this is your problem, then prepare for the stress eating. Create a stress basket. This basket will hold healthy foods, fruits, and other goodies that are of a healthier nature. They will have nutritional value and be low in calories. Stress is unpredictable. We all have experienced it and never know when it will strike us. Be prepared. Try to use the habit exercise to change an eating habit when you are triggered by stress. Perhaps that is the time you should take a walk, call a friend, get a spa treatment, or drink a cup of green tea. Doing anything that will soothe and comfort you will also have a positive effect on your body.

Be aware that your willpower weakens when you are tired and stressed. Most people have decreased willpower after a long day at work. Prepare for the evenings and low willpower.

Did you know that exercising, eating smaller meals a day, and journaling can boost your willpower? You can do it! Get out your journal and start writing.

Antiangiogenic Foods

The following foods have naturally occurring antiangiogenic substances. These are some of the foods that help to prevent cancer and slow down the growth of cancer. Include these in your diet daily: green tea, strawberries, blackberries, blueberries, oranges, grapefruits, lemons, apples, pineapple, cherries, red grapes, red wine, bok choy, kale, soybeans, ginseng, licorice, turmeric, nutmeg, artichokes, lavender, pumpkins, sea cucumbers, tuna, parsley, garlic, tomatoes, olive oil, grape-seed oil, and dark chocolate.

Healthy Recipes to Add Twice a Week

Tomato Sauce

Tomatoes are the only fruit that increase in their antioxidant power when cooked.

Adding tomato sauce to your diet twice a week will help prevent cancer.

Enjoy this easy recipe for tomato sauce!

Ingredients

Extra-virgin olive oil—coat bottom of fry pan, eight to ten tablespoons

Garlic—six cloves, chopped

Fresh basil—fifteen leaves

Fresh oregano—ten leaves

Tomato paste – one jar

Two jars of whole plum tomatoes— Crush the tomatoes
in the blender

Pinch of salt

Pinch of sugar or as needed

Dried Italian seasoning—one tablespoon

Directions

Heat oil in a pan. Add garlic and a few leaves of fresh
basil and oregano, and sauté over medium heat until
lightly browned. Add tomato paste, and cook until the oil
turns light red or pink (infused); add two cans or jars of
the blended tomatoes. Bring to a light boil, and add a
good amount (a handful) of basil and a few leaves of
fresh oregano. As oregano is strong in flavor, do not add
too much. Sprinkle a few pinches of dried Italian
seasoning. You can always add more salt, but for now
just add only a pinch of salt. Let it simmer for about ten
minutes. Taste it, and add more salt, if necessary. Then

pour over the prepared pasta. Finally, add fresh basil

leaves and freshly grated romano cheese.

Enjoy!

More Healthy Recipes @ GemmaHealthCoach.Com

Make your meals special. Set the table and light candles.

Try to eat together as a family as often as possible. Invite

friends if you live alone. Let your guest or family members

participate in creating the special meal. Remember to be

mindful and savor the food. Great food tastes best when it is shared with people you care about. Enjoy!!!

Eat a rainbow of fruits and vegetables daily

Exercise

Everyone has a different definition of "exercise." Some think they have to feel real pain for exercise to make a difference. Enjoy exercise. Make it fun.

If you have not exercised in a while, then do not go to the gym and burn yourself out the first week. Start by taking a nice walk in nature. Begin slowly, and gradually add more days. I want you to look forward to it. Have no guilt if you miss a day. Allow yourself to be human.

When you get to the point of daily exercise, try to have variety in each workout. You should include weights at least three times a week. Please be careful not to overexert and hurt yourself.

Did you know that jumping on a trampoline releases more endorphins that any other type of exercise? While you are jumping, the endorphins are very rapidly released and flow throughout the body. Endorphins are the brain's natural painkillers and are three times as powerful as morphine. Endorphins are also considered a natural mood elevator.

Jumping also releases adrenaline, serotonin, and dopamine.

Adrenaline is a natural substance that gives you a natural high.

Serotonin is the natural substance that affects your mood, especially happiness and well-being.

Dopamine is the natural substance that makes you feel cheerful and alert.

If the above reasons are not enough to convince you to buy a mini trampoline, then perhaps the great workout you will get from jumping will persuade you.

Try running in place or doing squat exercises.

Did you know that you burn 160 calories in thirty minutes by jumping on a mini trampoline? It is a low-impact workout, and it is so much fun!

I love circuits. Take thirty minutes and do three exercises.

Ten minutes on the elliptical, ten minutes on the bike, and

ten minutes on the rowing machine. Listen to music or an audiobook while doing your exercise, and enjoy the self-care.

Did you know that exercise releases endorphins?

It is the "feel-good" hormone. I call it a natural antidepressant.

Sleep

Sleep is very important for your body and brain to function properly. Most research shows that seven and a half to eight hours of sleep a night is required. Your brain needs to refuel. If you are not getting the proper amount of sleep, then you are not functioning at the optimal level. We are born with the natural ability to get eight hours of sleep a night. We are the ones who sabotage our sleep by consuming caffeine, watching television before bedtime, taking sleeping aids, and so on. Many of my clients tell me that they cannot sleep through the night. I say, "You can, if you work on changing that habit." These simple steps will help you sleep better at night:

Create a sleeping sanctuary.

Put shades on the windows to create darkness.

Put your electronics away from where you sleep.

Make your bed comfortable.

Avoid too much stimulation before bedtime.

Write about any problems in your journal.

Write your gratitude lists every night. (Studies have shown that writing gratitude lists before bedtime helps with proper sleep.) Make sure the last thing you write before sleep is something positive. Always write your gratitude list after you have written in your journal.

Problems: If you are struggling with problems, then allow yourself time off during sleep. If your habit is broken sleep and you wake up worrying, then change the worry time to during the day. Tell your brain that worry time is from 2:00 p.m. till 4:00 p.m. (or another time that works for you during the day), and then go back to sleep. You can worry every day if you want to; just limit the amount of time you worry, and try to enjoy the rest of the day.

Do the best you can, and trust the universe.

Day Six—Words and Assumptions

Today, on day six, focus on the power of your words.

Think back to a time when you assumed something. Were

you right? Do not underestimate the power of the spoken

word. Words have the power to change your life and the

lives of others in a positive or negative way. The words

that you say to yourself are just as important as the words

you say to others. Pay attention to your words. Follow

this rule: if you do not have anything nice to say, then do

not say anything at all. Honesty is important, and you

should always be honest, but there is a tactful way of

using words kindly.

Be mindful of your words today and every day. Pay

attention to your mind chatter and make positive

corrections.

Assumptions

Do not assume anything. You are probably going to be wrong more than 50 percent of the time.

A close relative of mine recently passed away. I was very sad, but I had to continue functioning in some capacity. I only did what I had to do. A very close friend called me and asked if I was doing any type of service. I told him that it was the wish of the deceased person that I not have a service. I told him that I would have a small dinner party in a few weeks to recognize the person's life. My friend did not contact me for the next four days, while others were visiting, sending flowers, and so on. I was hurt by his actions. My mind chatter was saying, "In times of trouble, you find out who your true friends are." I felt he did not care. When we did talk again, he said he was hurt that I did not ask him to come over. He felt like I was keeping him away, because I wanted to be left alone.

He assumed that he would be bothering me. I learned a lesson, and I believe he did too. We both cared, and we both assumed.

Do not assume, and do not ruminate. Ask the person what he or she is thinking or feeling. Clear the air, and shut down your mind chatter until you know the truth.

Day Seven—Play, Smile, and Hug

Make time to play, smile, and hug someone today!

I recently had the opportunity to observe my granddaughters at play. I watched them chase each other and scream with laughter. Their innocence and uninhibited demeanor captured my heart. At that moment, I realized how important carefree play is to the human spirit. I also wondered how many of us have play as part of our daily lives.

I started to analyze my own life and categorized my responsibilities and activities. The list went something like this:

Mother, grandmother, and friend—nourishing these relationships

My household responsibilities—upkeep and bills

The care and nourishment of my body—exercise, meditation, and healthy foods

My business responsibilities—clients and bills, including

continuing education

The closest thing I had to play was exercise. The sad truth

is that I know I am not alone. This realization prompted

me to include play as part of my daily routine.

First I decided to look up the definition. There were a few

definitions, but I liked the one-word definition: "fun."

Although the definition did not mention laughter, I

decided that I wanted carefree laughter as part of my

play.

I came across a study on the benefits of laughter. Not

only does it improve the quality of your life, it also burns

fifty calories for every ten to fifteen minutes of laughter,

according to a study conducted by Maciej Buchowski, a

researcher from Vanderbilt University.

In conclusion, remember to add play daily, even if it is

only fifteen minutes. Let your inner child have fun!

Smile, Hugs, and Mirror Work

Benefits of a Smile

A smile is a universal language. It is understood by everyone and so easy to do. It is not only a kind gesture to a stranger, but it also benefits you.

Many studies have shown that smiling every day can benefit you in the following ways:

Boosts your mood and increase confidence

Releases endorphins to help reduce stress

Produces a feeling of warmth and trust

Reduces your blood pressure and increases longevity

Strengthens your immune system

Helps you look younger

Lets off positive energy

The best of all is that it makes others smile too, and it is a free gift. If you are not in a good mood, practice smiling. It will boost your mood.

When you smile, even if you are not happy, you can fool your brain into thinking you are happy.

Types of Smiles

Jaw-drop smile: This smile is an exaggeration smile. Politicians and celebrities usually use this smile in order to draw a positive response from others.

The turn-away smile: This smile is playful, juvenile, and creative. Most men cannot resist a woman with this smile. They instinctively want to protect a woman when she shares this smile with them.

The closed-lip smile: This looks like the cat-that-ate-the-canary smile. It is playful, and it gives the signal that a person is hiding something.

The tight-lipped smile: This smile is displayed when a person smiles with a closed mouth and stretched lips. It is used when someone has a secret, is concealing his or her thoughts, or is restraining an attitude.

The lopsided smile: This smile is also known as the twisted smile. It is displayed when a person's lips slant upward on one side and downward on the other side of his or her mouth.

The forced smile: This type of smile is fake and unnatural. It is used when we want to pretend that we are happy. Although the teeth are shown with this type of smile, the eyes are not engaged and are dull and lifeless.

The sneer: This is the disrespectful or sarcastic smile. This smile shows contempt. This smile is created when the lip corners are sideward toward the ears.

The Duchenne smile, or genuine smile: This smile is a gift to yourself and others. It causes others to smile too. It is honest. The muscles around the eyes and the mouth are engaged when you display a genuine smile. You can practice this smile in the mirror by thinking of something that makes you happy and concentrating on engaging the muscles around the eyes. Once you have the eyes smiling, the lips are easy.

Try to use this type of smile every day.

(HealthWorks, 8 Types of Smiles and What They Mean | HealthWorks, 2014)

Hugs and Oxytocin

Get your dose of oxytocin daily. Oxytocin is a powerful feel-good hormone that is stimulated by hugging or kissing a loved one. Hug someone today, feel great, and make them feel great too.

There are other ways to release oxytocin too:

Touching (e.g., handshake with eye contact)

Watching an emotionally compelling movie or a scary movie

Singing

Dancing

Trying bungee jumping, roller-coaster rides, or other thrilling activities

Saying "I love you" to someone

Interacting with friends or groups

Doing or saying something kind for someone else

Mirror Work

Stand in front of the mirror. Practice your smile. You are going to be doing a lot of smiling. Watch how your face lights up and how your energy becomes friendly when you smile.

Stand tall with your shoulders back, and hold your head up high.

Remember, you are who you think you are. Walk into a room, and let the confidence from your stance be the first thing that others see.

Day Eight—Opportunity and Luck

Today, notice the opportunities around you. See what happens when you act on an opportunity.

There are opportunities around us every day. We have to open our hearts and eyes to see them. Talking to someone whom you do not know may lead to a friendship or business relationship.

Recently, I had to spend time with a very negative person for several days. I decided that I would not let the negativity affect me. I would remain my positive self, regardless of what this person said or did. After spending a few days with this person, I saw the positive change in this person's behavior. Every day I took advantage of the opportunity to talk to new people and try new things. This person saw the positivity surrounding me and the doors that opened for me. I was just being my natural self. By the end of our time together, I saw that I had the opportunity to make a positive difference in a negative person's life. I also felt the joy of knowing that I helped someone to now view the world in a softer, more positive light.

Take advantage of the opportunity to spread positivity by asking others to tell you something good about their life. Many people view kindness as weakness. That is a huge misconception. It takes much more strength and effort to be kind. Next time you have a negative encounter with a person, try kindness. You do not know what battle he or she is fighting in his or her life. Your kindness may make the difference in his or her entire day.

Today, on opportunity day, try to see the many opportunities around you, and act on them. You will be surprised about the joy you will get from opening up your heart to others.

Luck

We can all have good luck!

According to a ten-year study by Richard Wiseman, we make our own luck. In summary, the people who felt they were lucky had the following similarities in their thoughts and actions:

They all saw opportunities and acted on them.

They always followed their intuition.

They watched for flow and followed it.

They found the silver linings in unfortunate events.

And I would like to add that if there is not a silver lining, then make one! Good luck!

Day Nine—Character

Today is character day. We can all improve.

Does your character need a makeover?

Character is the individual mental and moral makeup of a person. The type of character a person possesses is portrayed though his or her personality, thoughts, words, actions, and moods.

The simple truth is that character is who you are. Your character becomes visible to others when you interact with them. We are judged by the quality of our character. You are only as good as your character, so let's work on making it great.

As parents, educators, and clergy, we try to teach children the right ways to think and act. Most religions teach good moral behavior by reminding us that there is a higher power and a judgment day. In the spiritual world, most people are afraid of karma.

Each day we are faced with decisions, and our character is tested. Most of the time, it is easier to do the wrong thing, since the pleasure is usually immediate. Who does not like immediate gratification? We have all heard the saying, "Hard work pays off" and have seen evidence that this is true. Doing the right thing has more value and pays off too. It just takes longer but is usually well worth it. Beware of instant gratification. The pleasure is usually fleeting.

Weak self-regulation and bad habits are components of bad character. The good news is that these character weaknesses can be strengthened if someone wants to. The key word is "wants to." Usually, the only way a person changes is if his or her behavior has caused enough pain. The great news is that both self-regulation and bad habits can be changed. Self-regulation is like a muscle that can be strengthened, and bad habits can be changed into good habits.

Take the strength test at www.viacharacter.org.

You can use this test as a guide to know your weaknesses and strengths and to make improvements where necessary.

Day Ten—Reframing Thoughts

There is a place for negative emotions. Just do not ruminate over them. This is where reframing your thoughts will come in handy. As you know, there is more than one way to look at things:

Divorce: This is a chance for me to have a new life. The old life and relationship was not working, and now I am free.

Financial problems: The universe wants me to figure out my financial life. What I have been doing has not worked, and now it is time for a change. I will have to make changes that can help me to get on the road to a better financial life. Tell yourself that you will take it one day at a time and one problem at a time.

Allow yourself to be human: On the first day of my certification course for positive psychology, I was so sick with an upper-respiratory infection. The class that day was on self-awareness, self-acceptance, and self-care. How ironic? My best strength is self-regulation and leaving early was not an option. The class was over at 6:00 p.m. and I made it until 4:30 p.m. that day and 1:00 p.m. the next day. I got the message, "I needed to allow myself to be human." It really helped me to say I am human, and humans get sick and need to practice self-care. What a great feeling! Practice being kind to yourself, and it will be easier to be kind to others.

A client had an ex-husband who would send her nasty e-mails in the middle of the night. She would wake up and read them first thing in the morning. We reframed her thoughts and labeled him as damaged. Only a damaged person would do that. She started to feel sorry for him instead of being mad.

Next time you have an unpleasant situation or thought, try reframing your way of thinking. Do not forget you are processing the event based on your life experience. If that way of thinking has not worked for you in the past, then change it until you like the results.

Take a step back, and observe your thoughts. Try to see the events through the other person's eyes. Maybe he or she has not had good life experiences and is acting in accordance with unhealthy beliefs. Maybe he or she is not trying to be difficult or hurtful. Give the other person the benefit of the doubt. Empathy is a beautiful and healthy emotion.

You are the master of your thoughts and life.

Day Eleven—Regret: Reversible and Nonreversible

Regret is a painful feeling. It is something that you have to come to terms with in order to live a healthy and happy life. Think about it. What do you regret? The process of cleaning up your regrets will help you enjoy a happier life. Use this worksheet to write down your regrets.

Regret

What do you regret?

_____

_____

_____

Why do you regret it?

_____

_____

_____

_____

_____

What can you do to reverse the regret?

_____

_____

_____

If the regret is not reversible, how can you free yourself

from the regret?

_____

_____

_____

The answers are all inside of you.

_____

Day Twelve—Relationships and Love

Today, we are going to evaluate our relationships. Evaluate the strengths and weaknesses in your relationships. Work on the weak relationships, and savor the good ones. Try to distance yourself from difficult people. They will drain your positive energy. If they are family members, then you will have to work on tolerance and avoidance of disagreements. Some difficult people are there in your life to help you improve and grow. Find the value in the difficult relationships that you have to keep in your life. There are positives in everyone. It may be a challenge, but try to find something good about everyone.

Relationships are so important to your happiness in life. The happiest people in the world all have strong, positive relationships in their lives. There are many different types of relationships. Each type needs work in order to stay healthy. Take a few minutes to evaluate your relationships. Try to make positive changes in the relationships that need improvement.

Parents and children: The "unconditional love" between parents and their children is a love of the purest kind. Although there are usually trials and tribulations during the different phases of one's lifetime, this relationship is one to cherish forever. Even in the cases where there is dysfunction, the parents are responsible for giving life to the child. If that is the only positive thing about the relationship, then cherish the gift of life.

Romantic love: Whether the relationship is between the same sex or the opposite sex, it is a warm feeling of caring. Love does not discriminate. It is a gift when you get it. The romantic-love relationship is valuable, if it is healthy.

Although unhealthy relationship are damaging they can be valuable too if you use the experience to learn and grow.

Twin flames or twin soul: This relationship is powerful and the most fulfilling relationship that you can have. The twin flame is described as the other half of your soul. You only have one twin flame. It is the ultimate relationship. When twin flames join, it is for some spiritual work. This relationship brings about spiritual growth and awakening. It is a very energetic and nourishing relationship. This is an evolved relationship and can only enter your life when you are a *whole person.*

Soul mates: Soul mate relationships are challenging and passionate. Two souls are brought together for a purpose. This relationship was predetermined. Many soul mates claim that there is a recognition upon seeing each other for the first time. These relationships are of the spiritual type and are often turbulent. There are usually breakups and pain and suffering. The end result is immense pain due to soul growth. Each of the soul mates has the opportunity to grow from the relationship. If they both do, then they usually reunite and sometimes have a successful relationship, because they cannot bear the pain of parting again. Sometimes one of the soul mates just cannot maintain the relationship, and the vicious breakup cycle starts all over again. The only way for a soul-mate relationship to work is when the soul mates are in enough pain to make the changes needed to sustain the relationship.

You have more than one soul-mate, so do not fret if your soul mate is not changeable. Before long, another one will appear when you least expect it. These relationships are so amazing when they are good. They are filled with drama when they are not. If you want less drama, then avoid the soul mate and pick a life partner.

Soul-mate friends: They are great relationships. I have been fortunate to have two soul-mate friends in my lifetime so far. You usually do not have all the drama that is in the soul mate romantic relationships. These relationships are usually quality. I like to say, they are a blessing from above. They come into your life when you really need them, and they help you get through difficult times. There is usually a dual purpose for the relationship. You help each other with the pain of soul growth. Sometimes they are only in your life for a short period of time to help you with soul growth. Send them away with loving thoughts. They are amazing.

Life partners: This is a comfortable relationship without all the soul-mate drama. Usually, both life partners enjoy each other's company. They have a friendship without all of that passion and breakup. It is a relaxed type of comfortable love without the spiritual agreement.

Friendships: You can pick your friends, so do a good job. Friends are gifts to yourself. No one is perfect, not even you, so take people on balance. Value the good in the relationship. Each friend brings something special to your life.

Pets: I believe I have had a soul mate, a dog. I met my dog when I went into the pet store to buy cat food. Buying a dog was the furthest thing from my mind. The minute I saw her, I knew I had to have her. I made the deal on the spot and have had a special bond with her that I never had with any other pet before.

Relationships are often tested when times are tough. Tough times are when you will see who offers support and who abandons you. That is a great time to weed your garden. Consider it a blessing.

Value, nurture, and appreciate all your relationships, and keep your heart open for new ones!

Day Thirteen—Flow

Flow is the natural progression that happens when all things line up correctly and the timing is right.

Today, we are going to look for flow and follow it.

Did you ever notice when you were trying to do something and there seemed to be roadblocks everywhere?

Nothing fell into place and everything was a struggle.

When there is flow, everything unfolds perfectly and effortlessly. You have to follow and look for the signs of the universe. When you feel a roadblock, step back, and reevaluate the situation. When you try to force something, you will get the feeling that you are rowing against the current.

Pay attention to the universe, and the signs that you are getting or not getting. Life is supposed to flow. We are the ones who complicate things. We do not pay attention

to signs.

The next time you feel a resistance in your life. Step back

and let the universe guide you. Do not force it.

Day Fourteen—Intuition and Spirituality

Today on day fourteen, start listening to your intuition. It is the wise voice that keeps repeating itself.

Intuition is the voice of your inner wisdom. *It will never steer you wrong.* The more you follow it, the stronger your intuition will become. The problem is that we do not always want to follow our intuition. We may want something that is not good for us, and we do not want to pay attention to our intuition. We start to rationalize and think that we can change someone or something. When we do not follow our intuition, we always regret it.

Start relying on your intuition today and every day from now on.

Today's Exercise for Intuition

Meditate for clarity and direction. Sometimes our intuition is blocked due to fear or stress. This is a time when you need to meditate and calm your mind. Before meditating, ask specific questions. The answers will come either during the meditation or shortly after.

Stay calm and trust that the answers will come.

Spirituality

People who believe in a higher power are happier overall—whether you get your spiritual fix from going to church, temple, or any house of worship. Your soul needs to be nourished just as your body does.

When I was in my early twenties, I told God that I wanted to know him. I chose to live a spiritual life. I have to warn you it does not mean that your life will be easier. It may be harder because your soul has to grow and mold.

Spiritual growth is painful and joyful. Usually, spiritual growth results from interaction with other people. It may be a soul-mate romantic relationship or another person who is able to touch you on a spiritual level for growth. Go with it. You will come out stronger and better when the growth process is over. You will have all that you need to get through it. People will show up to help you with either a kind word or deed. You may never see them again, but you will know that it was of a divine nature. Look for the spiritual signs, follow flow, and believe that you are not here alone. There is a higher power. It is an all good and powerful energy that we can tap into for support and guidance. It feeds our intuition.

Take a good look at the people who surround your life. They are an energetic magnet to who you are. If you do not like what you see, then start working on making the changes to become the person you want to be. This is spiritual growth.

Exercise for spiritual nourishment: Feeding your soul with positivity will improve your own energy.

These Are the Steps to Help Nourish

Try to stay away from negative things and people.

Avoid gossiping. If you do not have anything nice to say, then do not say anything at all.

Have an open heart and mind.

Practice faith and hope, and give and take love.

Nourish your body with healthy, unprocessed foods. The mind and body work together.

Meditate regularly, and expect and look for spiritual signs. Ask for them. Be specific.

Spend time in nature. I feel the closest to God when I am in nature.

Be kind to everyone. The kindness will mirror back to you.

Try to stay as pure as possible to feel closer to the higher power. Stay positive and surround yourself with beautiful things.

Most of all be grateful!

Day Fifteen—Fear

Today is conquer your fear day. Fear is the frozen

emotion. You cannot move forward. It freezes you in

place. In some cases, it holds you back in life. Conquer

your fears. It's easier said than done. Fears are real.

Let's get to the bottom of fear with this exercise.

What is your fear?

_____

_____

_____

Why are you afraid?

_____

_____

What are you afraid will happen if you do what you are

afraid of?

_____

_____

How do you know this will happen?

_____

_____

Write down the worst-case scenario.

_____

_____

_____

Write down the best-case scenario.

_____

_____

_____

The best way to conquer your fear is to just go and do whatever it is that you are afraid of. *Just go and do it.* After you have conquered your fear, write it down in your journal as an achievement, and give yourself the praise you deserve. Pat yourself on the back.

Day Sixteen—Organization

Today is organization day. Get rid of any clutter that you may have. Organize your home. An organized home will give you a sense of order. It is a cleansing effect.

Start by taking an hour today and each day to organize an area of your home that needs organization. Give away anything you do not want. There is a great feeling when you give things to people who need them. Do not look at the clutter and get overwhelmed. Make a plan on what you will accomplish in an hour a day. More than an hour may burn you out. After a while, you will get great joy from the accomplishment and the order that follows. If it helps you to hire someone to help you, then by all means do so. The desired result is organization. The way you choose to get there is up to you.

When you are all finished and organized, take a minute to savor the accomplishment. You can even take a picture to put in your Savoring Bank.

Day Seventeen—Visualization

Practice your visualization today and use visualization every day to obtain your goals and dreams. Visualization is a powerful tool to manifest the things that we want in life. Coaches use visualization with their team of players. There are two types of visualization: process visualization and outcome visualization.

Process visualization is the process that you will use to get what you want.

Outcome visualization is the process of visualizing the results of something that you want and working your way backward to get it. This is the visualization tool that coaches use effectively with their players. The outcome is to win the game. The coach visualizes the winning and then works on training the players to get the desired outcome.

Exercise for Visualization

Visualize something that you want to manifest. See yourself having it (outcome visualization).

Visualize each step that you need to take to get what you want (process visualization). Write the action steps in your journal.

Do this daily for ten to fifteen minutes.

Believe that you will have it too! Faith and action is a great combination.

Exercise to Create a Vision Board

Vision board: Create your perfect life on your poster board. Use magazine pictures, markers, and crayons. Be as creative as you would like. Do not hold back. When you are done with your perfect life poster, hang it up in a place where you can see it daily. Visualize your perfect

life daily.

Anything is possible if you believe!

Day Eighteen—Converting Emotional Pain and Forgiveness

Today is the day for clearing out emotional pain.

Emotional pain is a part of everyone's life. You can choose to suffer or you can work through the pain. This can be your most productive and creative time. Great beauty is born from pain. Embrace pain as an opportunity to learn and grow. It is a part of real life.

When things are tough, take it a day at a time, an hour, or a minute. *It will pass.*

Whether it is a tough day, week, year, or years, you will need to develop coping skills, and use the tools that we have already discussed to help you through it.

It is important to use reframing. Negative talk and thoughts will keep you in the rut. Make a positivity plan. Allow yourself time off from the pain each day. During your time off, do something pleasurable. It can be small, like going for a coffee or sitting alone in nature. Enjoying nature during difficult times is very therapeutic.

Create a support group of friends who you can call. When you need someone to talk to, seek out people with positive attitudes. If you do not have friends like this, then make some new ones. Open yourself up to meet new people. Sometimes the universe sends the most amazing people to help you along the way. Be open to the opportunity.

Gratitude lists are very important now. Write about the pain in the journal. I suggest that you do this at night. Make sure the last thing that you write is your gratitude list. During difficult times, I suggest that you write down twenty-five things that you are grateful for.

Help others. Divert yourself from your pain by helping other people who are in pain.

Use reframing tools for your thoughts.

Do not ruminate: When a negative thought enters your mind, replace it with a pleasurable thought. This will help to create a new positive pathway in the brain.

Join a yoga or meditation class.

Keep yourself busy.

Pray and/or meditate.

Use visualization to see your life the way you want it.

Take up a mindful hobby or activity. Knitting, needlepoint, putting together a puzzle, gardening, and volunteering can be a therapeutic escape.

Let your mind rest and be mindful. It will give you the break you need to refuel.

Get plenty of rest and take extra special care of yourself. Proper nutrition and exercise can boast your mood tremendously. Show yourself the love you deserve.

Change it up. When something is not working, make changes.

Use your history of problem solving as a guide. Take the

things that have worked in the past and use them.

Believe that you will overcome!

Exercise to Create a New Life

Draw a picture of yourself and your current situation. Use

crayons and construction paper. Be creative.

Then draw a picture of how you want your life to be. Use

as many details as you can. Details are important.

Now, write down a plan on how you are going to achieve

this life. Meditation will help if you are stuck.

Track your progress and stay hopeful.

Hope is the dream of the soul that can

become the reality.

Forgiveness

Today is forgiveness day. Forgiveness is the releasing of negative energy. It is a dual gift to the person you are forgiving and yourself, unless the person who needs to be forgiven is yourself.

Forgiving is essential in order to live a happy and healthy life. That does not mean forgetting what the person did. It just means that you accept that humans make mistakes. It does not matter if the person is sorry or not; you can still forgive.

Exercise for Forgiving

As painful as it may be, go over the person's behavior that needs forgiveness.

Remember there are two sides to the story, and you may not be completely correct.

Try to retell the story in a compassionate way, and give the person the benefit of the doubt.

Write a letter to the person and tell him or her that you

forgive him or her. You do not have to mail it. The letter

is therapeutic for you.

Visualize yourself giving the person a hug. If you need to

forgive yourself, then hug yourself and forgive yourself.

You are human, and humans make mistakes.

Commit to maintaining the forgiveness, and when the

thought of the person comes up, send loving wishes for a

happy and healthy life.

If you find yourself falling into the trap of being angry

again, then use your journal, and write about the event

and another letter of forgiveness until you are cleared of

all negativity.

Beautiful things can happen when you forgive.

Remember that forgiveness is a gift to *yourself*!

Day Nineteen—Life's Purpose

Today is the day that you evaluate your life's purpose. If you are already aware of your life's purpose, then see if you can build on it.

If you believe, like most people, that we all have a life's purpose, then it is important that you find out what yours is. You will experience a sense of fulfillment and great joy from doing your life's purpose.

For many years, I worked at a business that was successful; however, I knew it was not my life's purpose. I stayed because it created a comfortable living. I did what I had to do and what most people are doing. I am someone who wants to fulfill my life's purpose.

I am now doing so. Helping others gives me such joy. It is something I would even do without financial compensation if I could. I get a great sense of accomplishment and joy from seeing my clients happier and healthier.

Exercise for Life's Purpose

What is your life's purpose?

_____

_____

What would you like to do if money was not a concern?

_____

_____

Write down the things that you like to do and see if there is a way to make a business out of it or if you can get a part-time job doing it. This may be the beginning of a new career or a pleasurable outlet that makes you feel accomplished and fulfilled. Meditation can help you to find your life's purpose.

Day Twenty—Random Acts of Kindness and Volunteer Work

Today is the day that you do something kind for someone else. Notice how you feel after doing it. It does not matter how he or she reacts to your act of kindness; it just matters that you did something for someone else without expecting anything in return. Try to practice random acts of kindness as often as possible. It will bring you happiness and so much joy.

I was telling a friend that I have had trouble taking from people in my life but get such joy out of giving. One day, someone explained to me that I was being selfish because I wasn't letting the giver feel the joy that I feel when I give. I have learned to graciously accept a gift but still prefer to give.

Right after telling that story, I went through a Starbucks drive-through. When I went to pay, the man said the car in front of you just paid for your tea. Would you like to pay it forward to the car behind you? I said I would. He said I was the ninth car person that day who paid it forward.

I cannot tell you the joy I felt from the kind act and then I got to be the giver too. Double joy!

My Old Bench

The joy of giving can be addictive once you realize the benefits to others and yourself. I was selling my home and had put a "For Sale" sign outside in front of my house. I got a call from a woman who was interested in the old concrete bench in front of my house. I thought she was joking when she offered to buy it. I responded by telling her that it was old and worn, and she should buy a new one. I gave her the name of the place I bought the bench and forgot about the call. A few days later, there was a knock on my front door.

A young boy told me his mother, Nancy, was in the car and wanted to talk to me about the bench. I scratched my head in disbelief but walked to the car to talk with Nancy. She told me she loved my old bench and asked how much I wanted for it. I laughed and told her I could not sell it and that she should buy a new bench. We talked for a while, and I found out that she had seven children. Her husband worked during the day and spent his nights volunteering. She told me that she wished that he spent more time at home, but he was following his life's passion of helping others.

I was struck by the beauty in her face and the glow that came from within when she talked about her family. She mentioned that she lived in a three-bedroom house with her husband and children. Our backgrounds were very different as were our life experiences. I told her to take my old bench and that it would give me joy to know that she was enjoying it. She graciously accepted the gift and asked if she could visit me again. I told her she could but never expected to hear from her again.

A week later, I pulled in my driveway to find four pillows and a lovely note from Nancy:

Hi,

Wish I was able to catch you and say thank you again. We are enjoying the bench.

A little something for you to rest your head on.

Nancy

I am still so deeply touched by the beautiful connection. I never wanted anything in return and never expected anything.

Take advantage of the opportunity to give. This act of kindness will bring you so much joy.

Volunteer Work

Volunteering can be the most rewarding thing that you can do. It is a gift that you give others but actually a gift that you give to yourself most of all.

Benefits of volunteering: What does volunteering do for you?

Some of the benefits of volunteering include increasing self-confidence, mental health and life satisfaction. Studies have shown that people who volunteer have been shown to have fewer symptoms of chronic pain or heart disease.

Most importantly, it helps others and makes you happy! Take an hour or two a week and offer your time to someone in need. Studies have shown that those who do volunteer work add years to their lives.

It is about the loving connection that you give to someone

in need that makes you feel needed and joyful.

I assure you that volunteering will be a great addition to

your life.

Day Twenty-One—Vitality

Today is the day to evaluate the activities that make you flourish and feel vital. Do something today and every day that makes you feel vital.

What makes you feel positive energy? It is important for you to boost your vitality.

Here are some of the ways to

Meditating

Sleeping

Eating healthy, nutritious, and unprocessed foods

Exercising

Doing things that you love

Following your life's purpose

Make a list of the things that give you energy, and make sure you add these things to your daily life.

Twenty-One Days to a Happier and Healthier Life

You have completed your twenty-one days!

Congratulations! You have the tools to overcome

negativity and focus on living a positive life. Spread the

positive energy. For it is in giving that we receive. I wish

you a very happy and healthy life!

We Are All Connected

I feel compelled to share this story of an event that happened to me recently on the train coming home from New York City one evening. There are parts of the story that I have had to leave out to protect the privacy of the individuals involved, but I feel that the story is still worth sharing. I will be mentioning race and religion only because it is relevant to the story.

I was sitting on the train on a Saturday evening after a long day in school in the city, when a young black man chose to sit across from me. I am conscious of everyone when in public since I am a woman alone. I was curious about why he chose to sit across from me since there were many vacant seats, but I did not feel threatened. A middle-aged black woman conductor asked for his ticket. After looking at it, she told him that he was on the wrong train and that the ticket was not good for this ride. He apologized and told her that he was traumatized; he was from Baltimore and needed to get away. He told her that he was upset because his hometown was being destroyed by rioting. The conductor lectured him about asking for help when buying a ticket next time. I was standing by to pay for his ticket, if needed. I smiled at the conductor, and she smiled back. She said everyone deserves a second chance. I told her that she was a very good person. She smiled, sat down, and told me that she tries and that she loves the energy of good people. The young man told us that he had the strong feeling to come to stay with his brother in New Jersey.

I told him to always trust his instincts and suggested that he listen to the audio version of a spiritual book that helped me in times of trouble. The conductor said that she had read the book too and that it was a great book for him to read. I cannot disclose the name of this book for the purposes of privacy. I proceeded to tell him about a client who had an unfortunate experience with her son. Her son is an upper-middle-class, well-educated, white young man in his first year of college. My client got a call that her son was in the hospital for treatment due to police brutality. The young man had been drinking and was scared when two police officers approached him. He made the mistake of running from the police. My client had to drive a far distance to appear in court with her son for the charges. Although my client had tried to find out the severity of the charges against her son, the court said they were still deciding on how to charge him. They told her not to attend court and that the charges would be posted on the day of the court date; they refused to give her information, since the boy was nineteen years old. On the way to court, my client listened to the audio version of a spiritual book that explained how to use the spiritual signs to help get through life. She claimed that upon arriving at the court, she was calm and peaceful due to listening to the book.

Shortly after arriving at court, she was shocked to find out that the charges against her son had been elevated to resisting arrest and aggravated assault against a police officer. Apparently the police officer was hurt when he landed on his gun during the chase. The boy was facing one to three years in prison.

Just when my client started feeling all alone, she noticed a man in a suit walking past her. She asked him if he was an attorney. He said he was. She told him that her son was in a lot of trouble. He told her that he was the former prosecutor and would help her and her son.

The case was settled with the boy paying fines and also finishing a program for alcohol.

The point of my story was to let this young black man know that police brutality does not discriminate. It is my belief that if someone has the propensity toward negative behavior and the opportunity arises, then he or she is likely to act upon it. I wonder how many cases of police brutality do not get reported due to fear of public humiliation, loss of a job, or shame. I also wanted him to know that he needed to trust his instincts and follow flow in his life. When something isn't flowing, do not force it. The young man thanked me for sharing the story with him and said he would read the book or listen to it on audio.

At that moment, a woman came forward and thanked us all for the beautiful connection. She said that it was so nice to see people sharing and comforting each other. A few moments later, an older Jewish man came from the back of the train and said that he was the editor of that spiritual book I had mentioned. The words in the book were his. All of us gasped as we realized that this was no accident. A beautiful spiritual event was taking place. Four unlikely strangers were sitting together, sharing experiences, and comforting each other. We were all in awe at that moment. The older man proceeded to sit in our group and tell us that he was concerned about a health issue that he was facing. We comforted him and said we would pray for him.

The end of the train ride arrived. As I was walking off the train, it was bumpy, and I was holding on so as not to fall. The young man turned around and put his hand out to hold mine and help me off the train.

When you get the opportunity in life to say something kind or to open up your heart to someone, please do so. Beautiful things can happen.

A few points I want to mention: We did not exchange names. My client's son, the young college student, learned from the experience and is now on the dean's list at school. Always look for the good in a bad situation. You may not be able to see the good right away. It could take years before you can find it.

I want to offer a special thank-you to the attorney who cut his fee and made the young man take responsibility for his actions.

Do not miss an opportunity to say or do something. Listen to the strong voice that repeats itself. That is your intuition. It will never steer you wrong. Listen even if you do not understand in that moment. It will be revealed to you at the proper time.

You cannot take the journey for someone else, but you can offer kindness and support. The thirty minutes I spent with these wonderful people will remain a warm memory in my heart forever.

My class that weekend was on spirituality.

Make connections with other people.

We are all connected. We are not here just for ourselves.

I hope this book was helpful. I wrote it with love and the best intentions. I want you to be your best. I believe in you, and I know that we are all connected.

The power is inside you. Recognize and use it. Life is a journey. Make it a happy and healthy one!

Best of luck on your journey!

Live a Hopeful Life

Hope is the dream of the soul that has the potential to become the reality.

The following is a poem that I wrote several years ago. It is about life and hope.

Traveling the long corridor,

Weary, listless, worried,

All so common to the natural form,

Positive, waiting, ready to enhance the

arrival of yet another struggle.

Broken hearts, dreams, limbs, all those

carried through the years now lie heavy on

the back of the tired soldier of life's

constant wars.

The lessons learned were deeply embedded

in the soul, never to be forgotten,

The rewards hoping to be worth the never-

ending storm—

BELIEVING they must be...

Thank you for reading my book. I hope you have found it helpful and that you use these valuable tools that are sure to put you on the road to a happier and healthier life!

You have the power to create the life you want. You deserve to be happy.

Live a happy and healthy life!

Gemma Nastasi, CHNC, CAPP

About the Author

Gemma Nastasi is a fifty-four-year-old mother of three adult sons and a grandmother of four precious granddaughters. Her life's purpose is to help others live happier, healthier, and more productive lives.

Gemma received her certification in holistic nutrition in 2012 from the American College of Healthcare Sciences. After working with many clients, she realized that poor self-care was a symptom of a bigger problem. Gemma went on to study positive psychology and received her certification as a positive-psychology practitioner in July 2015. Her passion and devotion to her clients is evident in the feedback received from her clients.

She offers individual personalized sessions, group sessions as well as workshops. She is the author of *Happy, Healthy Life* (2014).

Gemma is also a motivational speaker, a volunteer for Life Choice Hospice, and a member of the Geriatric Advisory Council. She is described as talented by her friends and clients. She truly loves working with others and genuinely cares about her loyal clients.

Her favorite quote is as follows:

"The teacher comes when the student is ready."

Are you ready?

Contact Gemma or Check out her

Facebook page and website for

information on her services and the latest

updates on living a happy and healthy life:

GemmaHealthCoach.Com

gemma@gmmahealthcoach.com

www.facebook.com/Gemmaholistichealthcoachcom

28153723R00083

Made in the USA
Middletown, DE
04 January 2016